WRITING FOR LIFE: LIVING THE IMPOSSIBLE DREAM

By JH Haskell

WRITING *for* LIFE

LIVING THE IMPOSSIBLE DREAM

J. H. HASKELL

JH Haskell
Visit my website at www.jefferyhhaskell.com

Printed in the United States of America

First Printing: Dec 2018
Molten Press

To my wonderful wife without whom none of this would be possible.

INTRODUCTION: WHO IS THIS BOOK FOR?

I'm sure everyone would get some use out of this book. I've picked up a lot of knowledge over the last few years of intensely studying the art, craft, and business of being an author. However, if you're at a higher level than I am, then maybe you won't get as much out of this as someone who is just starting out. If you're not sure if you're at my level or above, you're probably not.

Those who haven't published anything, or are intimidated by the market, are going to get the most use out of this book. Think of it as the cliff notes of everything I've learned condensed into one easy to read volume.

You'll hear this a lot from me; nothing I say is set in stone. For every 'method' to succeed there are ten people who succeeded by doing the opposite.

This isn't a method. There are no magic bullets, anyone who tells you otherwise is selling something. There is no one way to succeed, but there a thousand ways to fail. What I say here is the way I succeeded, and it wasn't by accident. I had a plan and I followed through with it.

Why this book?

I've gone back and forth for a while on whether to write a "how to" or "help" book. The reason I finally decided was my friend Jim.

Jim is an aspiring writer. He writes hard sci–fi, and his current WIP (work in progress: see you're learning already!) is 140 thousand words long.

Jim asked me why I hadn't written a book about being an indie author when I had done so much to coach him and his wife into not only writing again but giving them a path toward success. Anyone can encourage you to write, but it's hard to find people who will encourage you to be an author.

Then I looked around at my life. They weren't the only ones. I was a cheerleader for my wife (who is a much better writer than I will ever be). I encouraged a friend who wanted to write, and who was sick of his day job to start writing. He isn't at the same level Jim is, but everyone has to start somewhere... and if you don't start at all, you'll never get there! No matter what you do in your life, time is going to pass. Whether you do nothing, or you do something. You might as well do something.

CHAPTER 1: ABOUT A BOY

A big question I always ask when I pick up a book about indie publishing or any other self-help book is this: Who is this person to tell me anything? Are they one of those hacks who make their money selling "how to guides" without actually ever doing the thing they are advocating?

Is he a nobody with delusions of grandeur?

Where are his books ranked in the Amazon store? Five million I bet!

Before I get in a ton of trouble with my fellow authors, let me specify the difference between a craft book, and a business book. This is a business book with some craft in it. Make no mistake, though, this isn't about how to be a better author, this is about how to be a successful author.

There are plenty of authors who are fantastic at explaining craft, in fact have a real gift for it, while their own books don't sell that well. The reason? If it was just about craft, you wouldn't need books on business or marketing. The truth is, it's never been *just* about craft.

Okay, here is who I am. It's a bit of a story, but I'm sure you will see yourself in it. From my experience, all of us writers have a few things in common. It's what makes us a tribe. It's why we feel a kinship for other writers and why non-writers sometimes don't understand us.

Let me clarify something, just because you're not published or indie doesn't make you NOT a writer. The only requirement of being a writer is writing. An author is how I refer to people who have novels available to purchase in a store (physical or electronic).

I learned to read on Amazing Spider-man comics. Seriously. I wanted to know what was happening so bad that I worked hard to figure out how to read them. I've never stopped reading since (or loving Spidey).

As I got older and my peers stopped reading, I started to stick out. In the ninth grade, I was reading Tom Clancy while the other kids weren't reading anything.

Of course, I flunked out of every English class I ever took. I was told I was a terrible writer, that I could never make it as an author with my bad spelling and grammar.

Even in basic training or when I was deployed during my time in the army, I always had a paperback on me. Boy how I would've loved to have had a Kindle back then!

What they didn't tell me, what I would have loved for at least ONE person in my life to tell me, was that story is the thing. Sure, grammar and spelling are important… to a point. No book is perfect.

But Story? Story is why people read. As I am fond of saying, they come for the story and stay for the characters (I probably didn't make that phrase up).

College, for me, was no better. I sucked at it. SUCKED. I had an English professor tell me POINT BLANK that I was an insult to the written word.

By the time I flunked out of college I was in my mid 20's, and life had beaten the dream from me.

Fast forward almost twenty years. I'm married to an amazing woman who is both encouraging and oh so smart! One day she looks at me and says, "Jeff, I don't think you're dumb. I think you have ADD."

ADD is short for *Attention Deficit Disorder*. I'm not sure what they call it now, or if they even have it anymore. It doesn't matter. The symptoms described me to a T.

Inability to finish projects. Inability to devote significant time to one task. Inability to stay on task.

I'd put off projects, even ones that paid me money if it meant having to work through complicated tasks. I'd often make small mistakes on long involved operations even though I swore I had done it right.

The list goes on. My wife made me go to the doctor, and he officially diagnosed me. Then he put me on the most common ADD medicine, Adderall.

My life changed overnight. That was 2011. Between then and 2014 I went to school and earned almost all **A's** for the first time in my life. I was asked by an English teacher I greatly admired, to be his assistant and help the kids who weren't as *savvy* as I was in English.

He thought I was savvy. Me. In English! **SAVVY!**

He was writing a book, and he wanted my advice on it. During this time I discovered the superhero genre and decided to try my hand again at writing.

I spent the next 6 months writing a superhero book. It's a trunk novel (a book you write then put away never to be seen) for a reason. However, I learned something important while writing it. I learned how I write a book, and it wasn't pretty.

During the winter of '14 money got tight. Like, I might need to drop out of school to go back to work, tight. Up until then we'd lived with my wife's parents and used our savings and the help of some relatives for me to attend a local community college.

One day a friend mentioned to me she'd seen some writing gigs on a website called Odesk (Upwork now). I figured, no matter how bad I was, if they were looking for creative writers on a contracting website, they couldn't be too picky.

I was hired to write a 10,000-word novella. I spent three months writing it, trying to make it perfect before turning it in.

Twenty-four hours after I turned it in he asked for another one... and one after that. Two more after that one. Then, the final one I wrote was a 30k historical romance set in 10th century Scotland. He didn't seem to care that my only knowledge of Scotland came from Braveheart.

Once I turned that in he asked me for another. At this point, I'd made about $800 total off of everything I had sent him. Bear in mind there were no royalties. I was ghostwriting (turning over all my rights in exchange for a paycheck). Over the course of five months, he had bought these stories from me, had them edited, and printed them.

Once again, my wonderful wife had a suggestion. If he could make money off my stories, why didn't we cut out the middle man and do it ourselves?

See why I married her?

CHAPTER 2: PUBLISHING? WHAT'S IT GOOD FOR?

That year I had a decision to make. Pursue publishing as a possible career or go back to work. I really didn't want to go back to work.

That's the year I discovered Chris Fox's excellent YouTube channel (see the references in the back). He did something called 'The 21-day novel challenge' where he wrote, edited, and published a book in 21 days.

For the next eight months, I woke up at 5am every morning. Listened to his podcast, along with a few others, and I wrote my fingers to the bone.

By July of 2016, I had 2.5 books ready to go and then I discovered the now defunct, Kindle Scout. I submitted my first book, and a month later I received the message every aspiring writer dreams of... "We want to buy your book!"

That opened a lot of doors for me. But, I was published under a pen name. I liked the books I'd written, but I knew I had a lot to learn. I spent the next year writing and learning until June of 2017 when I indie-published *Arsenal: The Full Metal Superhero.*

By then I'd made the USA Today Best Seller list as part of a box set under my pen name, but I didn't want to use that on the books published under my real name, not just yet. I earned it, but I wanted to earn it with a solo book before I put it on my covers.

Over the next year, I continued to learn, grow, network, and write. There's an old saying, dress for the job you want. Well, I hung out with the authors I wanted to be like. I befriended people like Lindsay Buroker, Chris Fox, Michael Cooper, Jason Cipriano and a bunch of other awesome, hardworking authors who all love giving back.

These are who I want to be. I learned something about myself in the process. It turns out, I'm who a lot of people want to be. Making 2-3k a month, even on the months I don't publish, and that's doing little to no advertising! I thought everyone in indie publishing was killing it.

I was wrong.

This is where I am now. Writing this book so that you, the unpublished writer can see a path, plot a course, drive yourself to success as an author. Not fame and fortune, but a living wage as a working author able to provide for yourself and your family. What you do beyond that, is only limited by your imagination and your willingness to do the work.

And oh God is there a lot of work.

CHAPTER 3: YOU'LL NEVER WORK HARDER THAN WHEN YOU WORK FOR YOURSELF.

True story bro. I used to think I knew what hard work was. What a joke. I was in the US ARMY fighting forest fires in Montana, and I thought that was hard.

Nuh-uh. Monday through Saturday, 6am (5am wasn't sustainable, I had to adjust my schedule), in front of my computer until noon whether I want to write or not. That is my schedule. I take Sunday off for religious reasons, but that is the only day I take off. It turns out, it's super useful to have that day of rest. I almost always come back on Mondays ready to go!

"What about your muse?" I fired her. She didn't show up for work a couple of days in a row, and I told her to take a hike.

If you want to succeed you have to be committed. Success for me was earning a living off my books. You have to determine what success looks like for you and set that as your goal. Aim high, it's actually better if you do.

It isn't just writing, though. Yes you do have to write every day (which translates to: whenever possible). I know there are tons of people out there telling you that you don't. That it's okay to take days off and go to movies and concerts and whatnot.

Those people aren't you. You want to make money. You want to be an author. You can do it, you just have to focus. Taking Sundays off is a personal choice, and I do recommend you take one day off from the actual writing. Just the *one*, though.

All those things you used to do, playing video games, binge-watching Netflix, that all has to stop. Either you're writing or you're thinking about writing, failing that you're reading about writing. Until you're making the kind of money you want to make as an author, that is your focus.

There's a reason I have an emphasis on money. It's a tangible sign of success. Making money isn't a dirty word. It doesn't make me a mercenary and it certainly doesn't make me a hack (even if my inner critic constantly tells me I am).

A lot of people, including some of my friends, didn't realize they could ever earn money as an author. They have their day jobs, teaching, lawyering, managing, and they thought maybe, one day, they might finish their novel and send it out to agents and who knew? Maybe they'd win the publishing lottery and earn a few bucks at it.

I hate to burst your bubble, but those days are gone. You're more likely to get struck by lightning than sign a six-figure deal with a publishing house. Actually, you are more likely to get struck by lightning twice.

On the same day.

One right after another.

I'm not saying you can't get published. I'm saying the chances are so small, the reward so minuscule, why would you want to?

Because you want to be a real writer? Let me ask you this... what about the New York publishers, who publish books by Snooky and Kim Kardashian, what about their opinion matters to you?

Wouldn't a reader's opinion be more important? Publishers have gatekeepers. Their job is to make you quit. Make you give up. Not because you're a bad writer or your story is bad, but because they don't have room on their publishing schedule to sign you. That's the reason they say no to 99% of all submissions.

"But Jeff, I want to be in Barnes and Noble!"

I'll tell you something, *every writer* wants to be in a bookstore. Have an endcap all their own. Tradpub or Indie, every one of us wants that.

Do you remember Borders Books and Music? How about Hastings? They're gone now and while I have no special ability to predict the future, I don't think B&N is long for this world.

Maybe a few years ago they could have stopped their inevitable fall, but now they are just hanging on. (I just checked ThePassiveVoice.com and there is an article about them trying to sell themselves).

What's left? What other reasons could you have? While you wait, while you think about it instead of do it, time is passing. Time passes no matter what we do, so instead of letting it pass and you're still NOT an author, why not let it pass and be what you've always wanted to be.

Live the impossible dream. Don't settle for just writing, be an author, make a living. Live the dream.

CHAPTER 4: MINDSET

When I first started writing this was a word I'd never heard before. A lifetime of government service and corporate meetings full of buzzwords and I had never heard this one.

Quite simply, this is the resolve within your own mind to succeed. I touch on this throughout the whole book but I wanted to devote one chapter to it specifically.

I want you to succeed. You want you to succeed too, right?

Wrong. Call it a subconscious desire for failure, or fear of success, or whatever you want. You, the writer, are your own worst enemy. You will sabotage yourself at every given opportunity.

Some people joke about how your house is never cleaner than when you're trying to write a book. Or how it's suddenly important to organize your garage. Then, there is a new video game out that you've wanted to play for ages. Maybe, an old game. Maybe a new movie, or binge-worthy series.

The list goes on. We translate these things as desires. I *want* a new game. I *want* to watch a movie. I *want* to stay up late playing (insert hot new game here).

What do you want more? Do you want to be a successful author or do you want to watch that show, play that game, see that movie, or stay up all night?

And it gets worse. Say you manage to isolate your impulses and not clean the kitchen or do laundry, or whatever is distracting you from writing (Note: I don't mean ever, just while you're writing).

Once you've slain that dragon, others will appear. You will *trick* yourself into doing things that *seem* like work, but aren't.

"I need cover ideas, let's see what's on Pinterest."

"I'll talk to fans on Facebook."

"I need to do some Marketing."

Some of these are genuinely important. Others are not. None of them are more important than the thing that is the key to your success: WRITING.

The Stanford Marshmallow experiment might be one of the most revolutionary, important tests of our time. In short, it measures a child's ability to delay gratification. The longer they can delay it, the more successful they will be in life.

Why is this important? We are at war with ourselves. Humans are wonderful at hacking their own psychology without even knowing it. We are actually brilliant at it.

If you're like most writers you're a creative type. You need to be creative to feel complete. That might mean knitting or it could mean DM'ing a role-playing game like Shadowrun or Pathfinder.

Those games are a lot of fun, just like numerous video games and visual entertainment. They're also a lie. They help you feel like you've achieved something, making it okay for you to not achieve anything else.

Have you ever wondered why so many video games have music and virtual fireworks to celebrate achievements?

It's for the same reason you give a dog a treat when he does what you say. It's training. We don't like to think of ourselves as Pavlov's dog, but we are.

You need to use this to your advantage and train yourself to write. Reward yourself when you succeed. Let your brain know that this thing you are doing, writing, is important and that you want to do it more.

What that reward is, I can't tell you. I do recommend it be something cheap because you're going to want to do it every day. Maybe buy a bag of chocolate and have a piece after every sprint. Whatever works for you.

You can learn a lot more about human behavioral psychology on the web, it's worth your time.

The funny thing is, just being aware of these dumb things helps us fight them. It's when we become complacent and go on autopilot that they all kick in.

Time to take back the controls!

My friend Chris Fox always has exercises at the end of his chapters and I'm going to shamelessly steal from him.

Exercise:

Identify two things that have virtual, but no actual rewards and remove them from your life for one day. Replace them with a reward only after you've finished your daily writing goal.

CHAPTER 5: GOALS ARE HARD

This will be a short chapter because it's easy to explain and oh so hard to do.

You need to decide what your goals are. There are a lot of different ones possible. Everything from "writing the great American novel" to "writing the story I've wanted to tell since I was a kid" to "show me the money."

None of these are bad goals. None. If you don't have any goals, though, you can't start. It's like a road trip. Where are you going? Where do you want to go?

This is going to sound like a bad job interview but I'm going to ask anyway.

As a writer/author, where do you want to be in a year?

In five?

In ten?

Make no mistake, those years will come and go regardless of what you do.

Once you have your long-term goals you need short-term ones. Studies show that goals motivate us, but only if they're achievable goals. For instance I could set a goal to be an astronaut. Simply having that goal won't help me. But, I could break it down like this.

1. Lose weight/get in shape.
2. Study for private pilot's license.
3. Take physics classes at community college.
4. Become independently wealthy so I can fund NASA so they will have astronauts again.

Okay, do you see what I did there? With the exception of goal 4, they are all very reasonable. I could even break them down farther if I wanted.

Let's take a look at my actual goals, shall we?

I want to be a mid-six-figure author. What does that mean? I want to make 400-600 thousand dollars a year.

Wow. Sounds far out there. While there are plenty of authors who do make that kind of money, there aren't a lot. Yes, I'm shooting for the stars. If I miss though... I'll still hit the moon.

That's too big, though. Too much for our puny gray matter to handle. Let's break it down some. What do I need in order to make that kind of money?

The inventive Michael Anderle has a theory. It goes like this, if you have 20 books and they all make $7 a day, then you will make 50k a year. I don't just want 50k, though. I want six figures.

I either need to have 20 books making $30 a day each, or 40 books making $15 or 80 books making $7.

If you want to learn more about Michael and his awesome ideas, his Facebook group is in the back.

Now I have some concrete goals. I need 40 books making $15 a day. If I write 4 books a year it will only take me 10 years to get there.

Okay, that's not good. It's not that I'm impatient… but yeah, I'm impatient.

I wrote 3 books in 2016 and 3 in 2017, and so far this year (2018) I've written seven (published six). At that rate I'm gonna be almost 60 when I start making the money I want to make. This brings me a new set of goals.

I need to write faster.

I'm not going to go into what that would take but you should see where I'm going with this. Breaking down your goals gives you a path. Paths lead to destinations.

Right now you're probably stuck on what I call "The treadmill of life." You're waiting for something and in the meantime you just keep trudging along.

Being an author is a journey. You can't go on a journey while you're walking on your treadmill. Time to get on the path.

Exercise:

1. Decide on a long-term goal. Where do you want to end up?

2. Break that goal down into years. What do you need to achieve by the end of this year?

3. Break it down by months. Don't be afraid to put numbers on it. Can you do a book every six months? Every four?

CHAPTER 6: ARE YOU THERE YET?

If not, why not? I'm pretty active in the author community. We're a small group (relatively speaking) and I like to hear what is going on. It's easy to filter out the things that don't matter. I don't post often because I like to wait till I have something profound to say. Well here it is...

You. Will. Never. Be. Ready.

What? You read that right. Like marriage and children, there are things about being an author that I can't prepare you for, both good and bad things. Sure I could list them, but until you live it, it would be nothing more than a list of attributes for an NPC.

The community (of authors) won't really exist to you until you're in it. You don't have to say anything (spoiler alert: most authors are introverts). Join forums, Facebook groups, websites, wherever authors congregate. Then, listen and learn.

I want you to know, that I believe in you. Sure, I don't know you personally, and that might sound hollow, but realize this: Every dream is possible, if you believe in yourself, work your butt off, and keep focused. It's like eating a large pizza all by yourself, you take it one bite at a time.

The difference between me and the ten other people who wanted to be authors and didn't make it? I didn't give it a choice. I chose, right from the beginning that there was no way out but through. I refuse to fail. REFUSE. I will change whatever I need to change, learn what I need to learn, do what I need to do, but by golly, I will make six-figures.

It's truly amazing what you can do when you refuse to quit.

That level is when you know you've made it. You can see it in people when you meet them. You can tell the ones who are going to make it versus the ones who aren't.

I look at the authors I want to be like and I can tell you they have two things in common.

1. **They don't quit.** Persistence will see you through a lot of problems.

It's tempting to quit. Especially if you used to have a really good day job. I have a friend, an incredibly skilled and talented author who writes Space Opera that is so good, it's hard to imagine why he hasn't hit it big. If he sticks with it, he will. It's inevitable. For right now though, he has to go back to his day job. He's still writing, but only time will tell if that is true in a year or two. I sure hope it is.

2. **They don't blame anyone else for their failures.**

When things go wrong you have two options. Find someone to blame or roll up your sleeves and get to work... Blaming someone feels good. It means you're not at fault. It also means, there isn't anything you can do to change the situation. You abdicate your power to resolve the problem in order to make yourself feel better. This isn't the path to success. Take responsibility, take ownership (I know it sounds like middle management) of the problem and work to resolve the issue and learn how you can prevent it from happening again.

Now, you might be asking yourself what kind of situation could arise? You're an indie author, not James Bond!

Here are a couple of things I've done in the almost three years that I've published. Anyone of which could have signaled the end of my story.

1. Upload the wrong manuscript in KDP and have the wrong book go out to readers.
2. Cancel your pre-order and lose pre-order privileges for a year because I clicked the wrong date.
3. Mistook 500 yen for 500 dollars and thought I was selling big in Japan (this just made me look like an idiot)

These are just some of the things I've done. There are a hundred more I've seen other authors do. Don't blame anyone else for failure, it does no good and won't help you succeed. We are all about success here. You must have a LASER focus on it if you want to succeed.

Exercise:

I'm not going to lie, this one is going to hurt. None of us are perfect. We don't write the way we want too. We need to realize that. Not in bad way, but in the self-evaluation way.

Pick one thing you know you need to improve on (dialogue, scene setting, POV) then, find a craft book on improving that skill and read it. When it comes to craft, I really recommend the traditionally published authors over the indie authors. When it comes to business, indie books all the way.

I am ten times the writer I was when I started. The reason isn't just that I write a lot. The reason is I'm constantly trying to improve. Everything I do is deliberate. Chris Fox calls it deliberate practice. I like that. That needs to be you. Everything needs to be deliberate. Including success. Otherwise, it's failure that is deliberate.

Trust me when I tell you, it is better for you to know your weaknesses *before* you publish. That way when the reviews start tearing you apart, you'll know ahead of time that they are wrong... or right.

CHAPTER 7: WHAT TO DO BEFORE YOU PUBLISH

There is a litany of things you need to do to prepare for hitting the "Publish Now" button. They're all pretty mundane, they just take a little bit of work. I'll make a list here so you can reference it for later. Not every task is mandatory but everyone will help you succeed. That is what this book is about, success!

1. Create a mailing list. This one is mandatory. I have heard about two-dozen authors lament not having a mailing list set-up when their first book went live. Don't be one of them.

2. Facebook author page. You hate FB, I get it. A lot of people do. 2.27 *billion* people use it. You don't have to have a personal page (at least not one you use) but having an author page and a group attached to

it will let you connect with your fans. You really want this.

3. Author Central. This is separate from your Amazon account. You need it to build your Amazon author page and link all your books. Each time you publish a book, you need to go to AC and claim it. This way Amazon knows it's your book. If you don't, when people view your book they won't be able to click on your name and see all the books you've published. This is **critical** if you are writing a series. You need each book claimed and linked on your series page so when the reader gets to the end of the book, Amazon knows to sell them the next one.

4. A professional website. At a bare minimum you need a good-looking, genre-appropriate (if you write sci-fi have space and planets) website for people to visit and sign up for your mailing list and see your books.

5. A blog. Do you like writing about writing? How about talking about books you like? If either of these things sound interesting to you, then go for it. You don't have to do this, but it can help.

6. A Goodreads account. Now, don't go look at your reviews on Goodreads, the community there can be brutal. But it is another avenue by which people can find you.

Things you shouldn't worry about on your first book.

1. Advertising. You really don't need to do any at this point. Just focus on your next book. If you like, start reading books about marketing. Seriously, though, don't spend any money on marketing your first book. Wait until you have a couple of books for people to buy.

2. Twitter. For the love... Twitter is a wasteland. Don't go there. If you're already famous Twitter is great, if not, you'll get nothing but people who are trying to sell something, bots, or worse. Just no. Don't go there.

3. Getting in bookstores. If you know an owner and they want some of your books, great, otherwise forget about it. That doesn't mean don't have a paperback, it looks good on your Amazon product page.

A note on spending time doing things that aren't writing. Don't spend a lot of time on them. There is a fantastic book called, *Never Check Your Email in the Morning.* I suggest you read it. The main point is this, the first thing you do each day should be the thing that makes you the most money.

That is writing, pure and simple. Nothing you do will ever make you as much money as writing.

Exercise:

Create an author Facebook page. Setup your Goodreads author profile. Setup your Author Central account. The rest of the things are optional. Do them if you want.

CHAPTER 8: WHAT TO WRITE?

This is a tough one, I can't tell you what to write. I could tell you that Dino-erotica (sadly that is a real thing) is the next big genre, and you should avoid Amish Cyberpunk like the plague. However, by the time you read this book there could've been a massive hit film about Amish hackers and then I would be very wrong.

I can't tell you what genre to write in or not write in, but I can give you some characteristics to look for. All I can do is show you the door. For a far more comprehensive way to break down genres check out Chris Fox's "Write to Market." It's an excellent book and worth every penny (not that he charges much).

Right now, the genres to avoid are the ones over saturated by books or authors and have far too few readers. K-lytics is a cool program that helps you determine this, but it is expensive, and I am a big fan of the zero dollar budget. Indie-publishing *can* cost an arm and a leg. It doesn't have too. Just like in life and video games, money will provide shortcuts but not guarantees.

The genres you want to look for should have the following things in common. I am going to list them in order of importance and go from there.

1. You must love it.

You heard me right. If you don't love a genre you have no business writing in it. I'm not saying you can't broaden your horizons, but for your first couple of books, write what you know. That doesn't mean life experiences, it means write about what you love. If you've been reading Teen Time Travel Mystery Romance your whole life, let your first book be that.

I can hear you now, though...

But Jeff!!!!! I want my first book to be a massive runaway hit!

I hope it is. If it is, please email me and let me know, I'll celebrate with you. I was at a convention recently where I was at a panel for high powered authors. Five authors, all of them making six or seven figures yearly. Of the five, three of them had massive hits in the first month of their first book.

I think that is great! The only problem is, those three authors can't tell you how to capture lightning in a bottle any more than Icarus can explain how to fly on wax-wings. The bottom line was, *they didn't know why they were successful.* It happens and God Bless them when it does. I hope they hang on to their money and parlay it into an awesome future.

The two I was interested in were the two who didn't have massive, runaway hits their first time out the gate. They wrote a book, then another, and another after that. They kept writing, kept working, kept improving and publishing. That is how you gain success. You don't give up.

Never give up, never surrender.

It was solid advice when I heard it on Galaxy Quest and it is solid advice now.

The next thing you're going to do is point to the hundreds of authors who have dozens of books and still aren't making it.

When people say it's a numbers game, they are only partially correct. All of what I'm saying, in fact, all of what everyone says on how to be successful, is determinate on you. Can you write a good book?

Yes? Great, now write another.

No? Figure out how to.

I'm not saying if you have books out there and aren't selling that you suck. If you have good books, good covers, good blurbs, and you don't give up, you will be successful.

If you haven't yet, don't give up. Giving up is the only way to fail.

2. If you want to be successful, you need to find a genre that is hungry for new authors.

    How do you know if a genre is hungry? There are a couple of ways. Like everything else it takes time. It would be impossible for you to step into the Amazon store tomorrow and know. You need to study the categories you're interested in.

You also want to avoid oversaturated markets. Military sci-fi is drowning in books right now. Even good writers can't get noticed because of the number of books.

3. Know your stuff! Whatever genre you end up writing in make sure you've read it. I mean *read* it. A hundred books? Not enough. 500 books? You're getting there. Not that many books in your genre? Then watch a lot of movies about your genre. You can never know too much about storytelling and your genre specifically.

Exercise:

Pick five books from five different genres and read them all. Easy!

CHAPTER 9: THE COVER

We're getting closer. You've finished your book, the next masterpiece in Amish Cyberpunk—right? Now what do you do with it? The next couple of chapters will give you an overview of the basics. I say, "the basics" for a reason. I can't explain the advanced stuff without you understanding the basics first. I may do another book down the road with more advanced publishing ideas, but for now, the basics.

This next part may be hard to swallow for some people. You've trusted me this far, I need you to keep on trusting me.

As children we are told "never judge a book by its cover." It is very good advice. It's also a flat out lie.

We always judge books by their covers. It's the only basis for judging that we have. On a book, a cover's primary role is to communicate genre and convince the buyer to click.

The fact that your character's sword is black or that the love interest has a thigh gap *isn't important.* If you hire a good designer (Not Fivver or Upwork) and you are paying an appropriate amount of money, then they should know what they are doing.

Most designers will give you a number of revisions for free as part of the contract. Don't waste them on superficial things that won't effect the sales of your book. Remember, the cover needs to communicate genre and peek interest. Telling the story is for the manuscript.

Look at the cover. Does it make sense? If it wasn't your book would you know what genre it was just by looking at it? That is job one.

The other job is to get the customer to click! You do that through color contrast. Have you ever wondered why so many movie posters are blue and orange? Seriously, Google it, the story is fascinating. If your characters are all in black and fighting a tar monster in the dark all the customer is going to see is a black square. A black square they won't click on.

After your designer... hold on a sec. You did hire a designer, right? You're not trying to do this yourself, are you?

If you're thinking you can save some money and do it yourself, let me stop you right there.

Unless you are a professional graphics designer with years of experience under your belt, you have no business creating your own cover. There are hundreds of cover design websites run by professionals with premade covers for as low as $29.99. No one can tell me they can't save up that money.

Success is about priorities. If you can't save up the money then that means you value something else more than you value your cover. When you put it that way... buy the cover.

A good designer will present you with options (and a contract). A good designer will try to make sure the character details are right, but *after* the cover does its job.

One of my favorite covers, *The Wraith (Superhero by Night)*, has a perfect image of the protagonist, Madisun, surrounded by blue light. It's awesome. It's just missing her signature red scarf she uses to hide her identity (superheroes do this). Why would I leave something so important to the character's identity out? The biggest reason is artistic. The red of the scarf and the blue of the energy didn't work together. The other part, is character. Between the scarf and the energy no one could see her face. It's hard to identify with a faceless entity.

The point here is, have some vague ideas of what you want your cover to communicate, then work with the artist to produce the cover that satisfies the business side first. It must convey genre and it must be click-worthy. Everything else is secondary.

CHAPTER 10: THE BLURB

I have bad news for you. You know that dream? The one you had where you are picked up by a major publisher and all you have to do is write?

That doesn't exist. I don't know if it ever did. Being your own publisher has its rewards and pitfalls. What those will be for you, I can't say. I can say this; I've never heard more authors bemoan one thing more than blurbs. They hate writing them. And most of them are no good at it.

Blurb writing is an art. One that you have to devote some time to be good at. Not, "spend your life on it" time, but at least read a book or two. Failing that, I can give you a primer on why blurbs are so important, how they work, and what a good blurb is.

Why are blurbs so important? When you are ranking things of importance for your book, it should look something like this...

Manuscript>Cover>Blurb>First Chapter> Everything Else.

A lot of times we indie authors become so wrapped up in talking about selling books we forget that books have to be good first. If your manuscript is riddled with errors, has a story that makes no sense, and characters that aren't engaging, then no amount of marketing genius will sell it in the long run. Oh sure, you might get lucky. But this isn't *Writing with Luck*, it's *Writing for Life.* Counting on luck is for playing the lottery.

When I was in the Army we used to say *better lucky than good.* That's true when bullets rain down around you, not so much when you're trying to build a career. You can't count on luck. You can't predict it. You don't need it. You need persistence, and time.

A cover will get your audience to your blurb, and the blurb will get them to either the "look inside" or the "buy now" button. How does it do that?

It piques their interest, then asks a question that makes them want to know more. There are two ways you can do this. *By telling the story of the book (the most common way) or by summarizing the feeling of the book (less common).*

I should also point out, there is a lot of genre-specific things that go into blurbs. Urban Fantasy favors first-person blurbs (personally I can't stand them), non-fiction has informative ones, action-adventure tend to be short and sweet. You get my drift. You know what genre you're writing in, make sure you do your homework.

The Story Blurb:

Until recently I favored this form of blurb. It is usually two-three short paragraphs. Each section has a purpose, like a book.

Introduce the Character.
Introduce the Problem.
Introduce the Stakes (what happens if the hero fails).

Like most authors writing "how-to" books, I'm going to draw examples from popular culture to allow everyone to relate.

Story blurb example:

Steve Rogers wants to serve his country in the largest conflict the world has ever known. WWII.

He's a runt, 4F in every way. No recruiter will take him, and the Army doesn't want him... that is until a former German scientist named Dr. Abraham Erskine, overhears Steve's impassioned plea to do the right thing.

Transformed into a super soldier, Steve Rogers must take on the mantle of Captain American and fight the Nazi's where they live.

Nazis aren't the only threat. Hydra threatens to destroy the world, and only Captain America and his Howling Commandoes can stop them. If they don't, the world will perish under the reign of the Red Skull.

This isn't the actual blurb for the movie, just one I wrote. It's actually a bit longer than the one for the movie according to IMDB. However, I think it illustrates my point nicely. It introduces the character, the challenge, and the stakes for failure. While also giving us a little bit of info about the villain. Notice what is not there?

Nothing about Bucky, Peggy, Brooklyn, his time as a PR stunt, when he went off orders to rescue the 107th... none of that is important to making the reader press the buy button. Less is more. Even more so in a blurb.

Now for the emotion blurb. What does Cap evoke? How does the movie make people feel?

Emotional blurb example:

Bullied, beaten, and denied his right to fight for his country, Steve Rogers is the last person who could win World War II.

He's exactly who we need and the only man who can.

A ton shorter. However, the hook is still there. How does he win WWII? Why is he the only man who can? Inquiring minds want to know!!!!

All blurbs, regardless of style or length, need to end with a call to action (CTA). Something to the effect of, "Buy now to start enjoying shield throwing fun!" This is psychology, trust me. Put the CTA in there.

CHAPTER 11: ONE BOOK OR THREE?

Trends change in the world of bookselling. You can go mad chasing them, but just because you shouldn't chase them doesn't mean you shouldn't follow them.

Last year LiTRPG sprang into the forefront with the addition of Harem novels. Trust me when I say, no one saw this coming. The year before that, it was bear shifter romance, the year before, military sci-fi. Who knows what it will be next year?

There are a couple of things that don't change, though. People like to read. When they find a book they love, they immediately look for more books in that series or by the author.

If you've only got one book out, and it's going to be a year before you have another, it might be in your best interest to wait until you've written all three before releasing the first one (I'll touch more on release strategies later in this chapter).

For me, I'm done with trilogies. Right now (and this might have changed so don't assume it hasn't) series are where my money is at. I'm on book 7 of Arsenal, and Book 2 of Wraith (as of December 2018). I plan on starting a third series and rotating the books so that my readers always have a new book from me to read, and I don't get burned out on one character or setting. However, they are all superheroes and they are all in the same universe.

What does this mean for you? There are plenty of authors who write trilogies and do fine and there are plenty who write stand-alone books (ones that aren't part of a series).

Any three of these are a viable path to success. However, stand-alone (stories) don't often sell well, so that isn't a good path to take. You have to rely on luck, and I don't like luck as a strategy.

Trilogies are much more viable. Releasing books in threes can jump start your career. Strike while the iron is hot. Once you release a book you have your best visibility over the next ninety days.

There are two lists for books. The list for your genres, and the Hot New Release list. HNR gives you lots of visibility because you're only competing with books released in the previous 30 days.

If you release each book a month apart, then you will have a book on the HNR for 90 days straight! That's a good plan. If your cover is right, and your blurb is tight, even a book 2 or book 3 can interest people to go check out book 1.

The last strategy, series, is one I learned from two really prolific and fantastic authors. Michael Scott Earle and Jason Cipriano. They start a series. Write book one, then start another series, then another. Then they rotate their series release four to six weeks apart.

It would look something like this. Jan (Book 1) Feb/March (Book 1) April/May (Book 1). Then Book 2, so on and so forth.

This strategy has several advantages. One, it keeps your books and your name in the limelight. Two, you won't get burned out writing a single series. Three, if any series dies out, or doesn't start, you can kill it and still have two other series out there while you start another.

What's the drawback? A couple. One, and this is a doozy, you have to be able to write fast. How fast? Four-to-six *thousand* words per day. Assuming you work six days a week (which you really should when you're first starting out) that gives you a solid 70k-80k book a month.

Two, you need to be comfortable releasing books with minimal revision. This is a deal breaker for a lot of people. I'm going to expand on this idea a little later, so if it is repellent to you, try to keep an open mind and hang on.

If this doesn't work for you, or can't work for you, find a way to alter it and adapt the ideas so you can. The more often you release, regularly and reliably, the faster your audience will grow. A book a month is a goal few people outside of the incredibly skilled romance authors can pull off. I have yet to achieve this, and I write every day, four-thousand words a day minimum.

I built my audience releasing a book every three months, four on the outside. You see, the readers you want, the really loyal readers who buy every book you write and talk to their friends about you, they read a lot. They can't remember all the authors they read. If you take six months or a year to release the next book, they will have forgotten about you. Don't let them forget about you.

There are other release strategies, these are the three I see succeed time and time again. Adapt them to what works for you, make a plan, and execute the plan!

Exercise:

Read 2k to 10k by Rachel Aaron and follow it up with 5,000 Words Per Hour by Chris Fox. Spend a week practicing what you learn. You should know by then how fast you can reasonably write.

Addendum: You don't necessarily need to write fast. My friend Michael Cooper (MD Cooper of the Aeon 14 series) is a self-proclaimed slow writer. He just spends eight hours every dang day, writing and usually hits about 12k a day.

CHAPTER 12: KEYWORDS

I bet you thought the next thing was publish... nope. I'll tell you, I spent a lot of time trying to demystify keywords. If you have a background in Internet marketing, then you may know more about this than I.

Keywords are search terms. When you go to Google and type in, "What about Bob, movie?" each one of those is a keyword.

Amazon gives you seven keyword spaces. Despite it saying 'keyword' it is actually phrases. You can put more than one word in each box.

They tell you not to put genre and other duplicate things from the cover in the terms... I don't know why they say that. The only way to get in certain genres (Teen superhero for example) is to have the keyword "Teen Superhero" in the keywords. I speak from experience here. Arsenal (Book 1) had the words "teen protagonist" in the keywords and "Full Metal Superhero" is the series name. Despite that, it wasn't until almost seven months after release that I discovered it wasn't in the teen superhero category and I had to request KDP move it. They did.

My point is, more is better on the keywords. Keep them generic but also on point. "Thriller" by itself is a terrible keyword. But, "Immersive Psychological Thriller" is excellent.

One more thing... ALWAYS READ THE GUIDELINES OF THE ALMIGHTY 'ZON. If they say "we don't recommend," feel free to ignore it (if you think that is best) if they say "It is against the TOC (rules)" then don't frigging do it. Just, DON'T. People who cheat the system hurt all of us, and the only reason most of us have a career is because of Amazon ('Zon). Let's not turn them into an enemy.

CHAPTER 13: THE MINUTIA

There's a lot of it. You need to upload your manuscript (formatted for ebooks and a different one for paperbacks). You need to have your cover fit the right dimensions (again for both ebook and paperback).

Then you need to address copy protection, rights by country, pricing, and if you will be in KDP Select or not.

If you're new, just starting out with your first book on the horizon, then I wholeheartedly recommend KDP Select (to the consumer it's known as Kindle Unlimited).

There are as many opinions on this as there are authors. Few agree. Most would say it is good (like me) others will say it is the doom of the indie author.

I don't know the answer. About 30% of my income comes from page reads (how they pay you, each page is assigned a value by Amazon, the total number of pages from your books read in a month, times that value is what you are paid). On average, a hundred thousand page reads ends up being about $400.

If you write longer books it's in your favor. If you're like me and you write series that release every few months (or sooner) it also favors you. However, there is no magic boost KDP Select gives you. When I say it favors you, I mean the way the system is built. Long books earn more money per book. Books that release quickly stay on the HNR list, that kind of thing. There isn't any arbitrary advantage. Many authors will tell you things like this, and they just aren't true.

After you choose those options you're left with one more. I swear this is the last choice you have to make before hitting the "Publish Now" or "Submit" button.

To pre-order or not to?

Exercise:

Go through the KDP control panel on a "fake" book. It won't hurt you just to hit the "+" button above ebook. Do this well in advance. I don't want you stressing out about your first title while also navigating KDP dashboard for the first time.

CHAPTER 14: PRE-ORDERS, WHAT ARE THEY GOOD FOR?

I would say the second biggest controversy (after KDP select) is pre-orders. Some authors swear by them, some hate them.

Regardless of what you choose, there are advantages and disadvantages to each.

For the love, if you do decide to do a pre-order, MAKE SURE you have enough time to finish your book, get it to the editor, get it back and make changes, have it proofread then submit it to the KDP dash.

Half the problems people have with pre-orders is that they don't give themselves enough time to finish the book. You can only schedule them out 90 days. If you are sure you can have it done, I mean sure, schedule it out.

How far out? As far out as you feel you can do to help drum up sales. I like one-month pre-orders. With a month you get your book in the HNR list for 60 days. The thirty it's on pre-order and the 30 after it is released.

You can use those thirty days to drum up some advertising, do giveaways, talk about your book on Facebook, etc.

Things you shouldn't do? Don't put off finishing the book to the last second. This isn't high school or college, there are consequences for missing that pre-order date. Don't do it.

Don't tell your friends and family about it. You want the holy grail of readers, *organic.*

Remember when I was telling you that your cover needs to scream your genre (literally if you can swing it)? This is why.

There are people out there who are looking for *your* book. That's right, the book you wrote. The only way they will ever find it (assuming you aren't rich and can have

TV commercials) is if they are browsing a category they want to read from and they see your book.

Think about all the times in your life you've gone looking for a book to read. Regardless of if it was on Amazon or making a trip to B&N, you probably didn't go there thinking, "I need that new Jeffery H. Haskell book!"

No! You went in with the idea of buying a book from a specific *genre.* You wanted a cookbook, or a sci-fi, or a travel guide, sword and sorcery... you get my point.

People browse the 'Zon the same way. They use the categories to find the genre they want and then they start scrolling. If your cover jumps out from the computer/phone/Kindle screen as exactly what they are looking for, you've got yourself a sale.

This is what pre-order is for, it gives your audience the opportunity to find you.

Now, if you tell your mom, sister, cousin, boyfriend's cousin, and they all run out there and buy your book, it's going to make a mess.

Go to any book in the store and look under it. There is a section recommending similar books. This is how Amazon sells books. If you like "Murder on the Space Shuttle" you may also like...

If all those people you told to go buy your book (by the way, none of them will read it. I don't know why but it seems to be almost universally true that friends and family don't read your work) then your also-boughts for your Amish Cyberpunk will have cookbooks, travel guides, self-help etc. Amazon won't know who to show it to. So you won't appear on anyone's also-boughts.

Like Fox Mulder, I believe. I believe they are out there and they are looking for you. Help them find you. Help them, help you!

Exercise:

Go to any genre but make sure you also visit yours, and look at the HNR list and see how many books are on pre-order. What's their ranking? Do the covers look like other books in the genre?

CHAPTER 15: HIT THE BUTTON!

Hit the button! Do it now. You've checked and double checked, you have your single book or trilogy ready to go. Your author page, Facebook page, and email list is ready to go. All of them are linked in the back of your book and ready for readers to click on. You have an outstanding cover that SCREAMS your genre and you have a blurb so enticing, so dramatic, people will click on it in droves.

Stop waiting and start doing. Hit the button.

Did you?

Do you feel like vomiting?

Yeah that's just about everyone on their first half dozen books.

I won't lie, it gets easier, sometimes. Sometimes it's worse. It's hard to tell. Nothing was ever as bad as the first one though. I really did think I was going to vomit.

If you feel totally calm, awesome. I envy you, but if you're like 99% of everyone else, you are feeling perfectly normal for the situation. A mix of fear, panic, and fight or flight. Maybe just flight.

CHAPTER 16: EUREKA!

I was going to call this "What should my launch look like," but that seemed too long.

You've hit the button. Launch day has come and gone, what do you do?

Besides working on your next book, if you're like every other author you are glued to your KDP dashboard and either cheering every time you get a sale, or groaning when you don't have one.

You might be left wondering why your book isn't selling, or why it's selling but not very much. These are all good questions.

They are also questions that don't have answers. No one can tell you why one book will sell like hotcakes while another doesn't move at all.

Not traditional publishers, not indie authors, not gurus. Sometimes lightning strikes and sometimes it doesn't.

Which brings us back to luck. Luck, isn't a plan. One of the hardest things you will ever do, and one of the most critical things, is to divorce your emotions from your book. You can't do it completely, but you can try. Please do.

Once you can look at your book objectively you can analyze some of these things. If your book isn't selling at all, the most likely culprit is the cover or blurb.

There are plenty of groups on Facebook who will help you workshop it. Think carefully before you pay anyone to help you with anything.

Don't forget, if it's too good to be true, assume it is.

If your cover and blurb check out, then go to your look inside. Is your first line gripping? Does the first chapter keep and hold your attention? This is where emotionally divorcing yourself comes in handy. The author in you will say, "Yes, my first chapter is essential!"

Is it?

Odds are it's one of those things. There is a path that readers follow when they search for books. They go to the genre they want to read in, then they look for a cover that interests them. If they click on it, sometimes they'll buy the book without reading the blurb, but more often than not, they read the blurb.

This is the path. If they aren't buying your book it has to be one of those three things.

Let me repeat this. It *HAS* to be one of those things. There isn't anything else for them to not like. Are you starting to see why the right cover is so critical? Forget everything else, if your cover doesn't NAIL it, then no matter what your blurb is or how good your first chapter reads the readers will never get there.

If after careful study all three things are as good as you can make them, then there isn't really anything you can do for this book.

Don't throw away good time after bad. Learn what you can learn and move on. I don't suggest spending a lot of time trying to fix your first book. Don't re-write it, don't republish it, just move on.

Now, what if you are selling 1 copy a day (assuming you're not in KU) then you're doing good. There are a lot of authors who don't sell that many books in a week.

If you are in KU, then add 300 page reads a day (depending on book length) and you are doing good. This may not seem like amazing numbers, but they are.

If you visit Facebook forums like 20Booksto50k or the IndieAuthorSupportGroup you will read about dozens of authors who aren't selling any books.

Any. As in, zero. Make no mistake, success isn't easy. If it was, everyone would do it!

At thirty books a month and 300 page reads per day, assuming you're selling your book at the Amazon suggested price of $2.99, you're looking at an average of a hundred dollars a month or $1,200 a year.

Any more than that and you are doing fabulous.

Bear in mind, that is better than ZERO. Which is where you would be if you hadn't published. I never said it would be easy, in fact, I think I said the opposite of that.

Don't despair or celebrate yet. The job's not done.

One book doesn't a career make. You may not be happy with your sales or you might be through the roof. Regardless, your next move doesn't change—

Put this book down and start writing yours.

REFERENCES

Why are there no links?

The short answer is this, some retailers (Apple) don't like it when you link to anyone but them. In order to publish on that retailer (Apple) I've had to remove all links. There are websites like Books2Read that will generate universal links, but I've seen many of those sorts of things go out of business. I'll trust you can do a Google or Amazon search without my help!

Authors to Follow

Lindsay Buroker
Chris Fox
Michael Cooper

Podcasts for Research.

The Science Fiction and Fantasy Marketing Podcast
Chris Fox's YouTube page
The Creative Pen
The Self-Publishing Formula

Take these with a grain of salt. There are a lot of opinions out there in the world. Try to listen to the people who have some success to justify theirs and avoid the people who don't.

20Booksto50k
Indie Author Support Group
Indie Author Cover Project

A QUICK WORD ON SCAMS

There are no magic bullets, no systems, no author who can promise you anything. They will, believe me, they will promise you the sun and the moon! By the time you realize they can't deliver, they already have your money. Trust your gut if it says "Danger Will Robinson, Danger!" Don't be afraid to reach out to other authors and ask for references. Don't be afraid to drop me a line and ask.

Afterword

That's it, the whole shebang. Every piece of useful advice I've received over the last two years condensed into this manual.

I want you to succeed. On that note, if you have any questions, want clarification, or just want to talk with me, join my group that I created for this book alone.

https://www.facebook.com/groups/584203725341415
or see me at my author page...
https://www.facebook.com/jefferyhhaskell

If you want to be an author, if you want to turn your dream into a living, I want to help and I'll do everything I can to do so. (Note: I don't charge for access or any crap like that).

If you're interested in reading my fiction, check out my superhero series here—

Arsenal (The Full Metal Superhero)
The Wraith (Superhero by Night)